HOME MOVIE NIGHTS

By the same author

PENN
(Raven/Thistledown)

HOME MOVIE NIGHTS

SARA BERKELEY

Raven Arts Press/Dublin
Thistledown Press/Saskatoon

HOME MOVIE NIGHTS
is published in 1989 by

THE RAVEN ARTS PRESS   THISTLEDOWN PRESS
P.O. Box 1430   633 Main Street
Finglas   Saskatoon
Dublin 11   Saskatchewan
Ireland   S7H OJ8, Canada

ISBN 1 85186 050 9 (Raven)
ISBN 0 920633 59 5 (Thistledown)

Raven Arts Press receives financial assistance from The Arts
Council (An Chomhairle Ealaíon), Dublin, Ireland.

Thistledown Press acknowledges the financial assistance of
The Canada Council and the Saskatchewan Arts Board.

Canadian Cataloguing in Publication Data

Berkeley, Sara, 1967 —
   HOME MOVIE NIGHTS

   Poems
   ISBN 0 920633 59 5

1. Title
PR6052.E74H64 1989 821'.914 C89-098055-1

Designed by Dermot Bolger & Aidan Murphy.
Cover design by Susanne Linde & Dermot Bolger.
Front cover photo by Connor Tilson.
Back cover photo by Podge O'Farrell.
Printed in Ireland by Future Print Ltd., Baldoyle.

CONTENTS

For Simon, Steve & Jon

I

LITTLE RIVER

When harm is done
Your sorrow
Creaks along like an ice-floe
And then it is no man's remorse
But a hunted animal
Tangling in briars and tearing free
On and wantonly on from the small wrong —
But I can be a river where the scent will drown.
I am the river where you come to fish,
Lean and fleet where the line drops lazily in
Trembling with the slight fish just below my skin
And where the threaded fly brushes
    winnowing riverweed
My warm current carries the light twig
And the small wrong
Downstream, and above me on the wooden bridge
You swill water in the pail,
Ready for all I have to give.

LESS THAN A HUNDRED HOURS.

I have put on a warm skin
I have come in
From the garden, where a pallor is caught
On every thorn.
You know it's you I see at evening
Before the light goes.

The secret alters with the hours
Sleep slows the colours
But in the morning, waking from some warm place
It flowers timidly against the covers
Pale on the pillow where six hours of sleep
Damp down easily to a drawing of breath.
You know it's you I see at evening
When the light goes.

It is less than a hundred hours
And the secret fits so close I have almost grown to it,
Something I have touched a lot,
I know its shape by every light
Its colours deepen as the day arches
Towards noon,
Dragging its heavy form
By night it has become
Hot and damp in the palm
And now it is less than a hundred hours
Until you come.
You know it is you I see at evening
Before the light goes.

A CHANGE OF NAME
(For the first day of spring)

The first flying thing is in the room
Without ever entering
Windows unseal themselves
Yawning outward
There's a restless yearning of small leaves.
Don't speak of awakening,
   there could be no such thing
When the pulse flew too red for sleep
The glow warmed too well
For cool rest - speak instead
Of a change of name
Sit tightly on the old self
And see the dispossessed
Wander lightly around the room
Hover a while in the faint human air
And not hearing anyone's name
Blow quietly out
Until it is no longer there.

LEAF DANCE

I take a leaf dance down the avenue
I who am named for clouds,
Whose rains soon dry.
The rhythms let me close my eyes
I walk on rivers when they flow
This deep and still
Through heavily green-drugged land
Where hills are smudging into a sky
That is letting go;
Trees secret all the warmth there's been
Darkly about their limbs, a shallow calm
Settles on the birds, among whom
None sorrow.
I feather out, as though
Supports were being removed
A cold wind is getting through.
A shock of geese
Goes up with a grace I have never known
Their arrow skims the coming night
Shot to the moon; they take with them
All the day's loose shame,
And the guilt that fits like another limb.

A STUDY OF US TOGETHER
(For Niamh)
This is how I go with her,
You can study us together,
We listen to the water notes
That tremble down the ear's tunnel
We hear
The spring's first impulse to tears
That is checked by the wind's sigh,
We both get washed away
On the wild silk, moonroll of Spring tide
My sister and I.

The same anvil beaten and beaten
Until the shape is white-hot beaten,
You can carry away this fashioned thing
And it is not love
But stuff of the marrow and nerves
And of the blood.
Sometimes we are two notes
A breathspan apart - the breath of a tiny bird
With the hint of a minor tone beneath his heart,
Sometimes one is shorter,
We are sometimes both the same,
        and how easy to citizen
This world of two notes
With the faintly minor beat of wings
And a brave face put on things.

Sometimes we listen
To ghost notes making the memory tremble
And the room is washed through
Washed free of all trouble, and we
Are two small girls again, eating ice-cream,
We could be any age,
Seven, eight, nine.

TEN

Her tenth birthday
Sends an ache from eye to eye
Across my brow she strings the decade
She has made; down my spine
Her lovely fingers let the years course through,
A pool forms at the base.

Double-figured, she unwraps her gifts,
Turning up her tiger-lily face, freckled, sure
Of a rich capacity to please
And if a sudden impulse should arrest
My empty lap
To gather her in
My shoulders to have her weep at them again
I wonder could I keep her in the dark
Where she would lean only to my sun;
But when she sleeps she seems to briefly
Join the dead
Taking on their ice-edged white
Not to be touched
In case a flaw should shoot across the skin.

Even taking her leave for school she takes too much;
I wish her well,
She swallows the wish,
A slim match, eating her flame,
Archly blackening,
So I offer her the gift of choice,
She chooses lightly with her delicate hands;
An hour of silence, poppy seeds, the tale of Ruth,
Such things.

Allowed out on her own
She comes in, wind-blown,
Arms full of contradictions,
Laughter about the eyes
With their mute agreement of grey and green,

18

She should have been named
For a queen
For she loves to presume,
She does it with a simple calm
Counting mountain peaks among her natural heights.
These rumours reach me by a side-wind:
I never gave her leave to grow
So leggy-geranium tall.

Once she raised the lid on a box of light;
Her face dazzled, and I thought I saw
A child of light - but in a waking dream
She let it close again; has no-one seen
How a little light
Still plays about her when she smiles?

WE GET ALONG

We get along like two
Houses on fire. We burn excitedly,
Swopping flames, crackling with joy —
Let it always be so,
O let it always.

I'm tired of going round and round,
My tail in my mouth;
Every revolution makes me fear
I've always been wrong
About everything;but we get along
Like two houses alight
And spitting stars, our laughter
Is less of a secret,
More of a shout
Into the endless, flame-shot
Night.

SCARECROW
(For John)

I danced with a man of straw
The music blew through his prickly arms
His heart was a reed
It went with the wind,
His smile was wry, tinderish to the touch
There were seeds for teeth
I could hear the pods cracking
As he lit a song.
We danced for a week, I was danced dry
I heard the changes being rung in me
And had I been a bird
I, too, would have risen with a shrill, vowel sound.

POLE-BOUND

Pole-flown, jittering in the sun
You can see me for miles
I am the jubilant one
Highflown; my spirits soar and whip,
Knuckles white, I grip the wind.
We are bound. We are all thoroughly bound.

I have all this wasted passion
And how do I sleep?
The restless breezes paw me awake
My tongue is minced, it ripples uselessly,
I am the one who always sees the dawn.
I sleep fitfully.

Rain moulds me, abject,
To the bitter pole
I brush my eye-lashes wearily against its cheek,
Yes, this is reluctant love,
Everything's under lock and key
In my heart. Everything's shut down.
I can see for a hundred miles around
But I am bound. We are all closely bound.

JUST DON'T WALK OUT IN FRONT OF MY BIKE

Don't walk out in front of me
When I'm pedalling so hard,
Quite likely to cycle over some edge,
Because I could take you too
Or you might unhinge the symmetry of my
Beautiful, clear-eyed bike.

You ran me over with your passion for fast cars.
You know, you are
Only one of the men I know
And in my own, shy way
I like them all; you scorched me slightly
With your fire-fascination, but I was right
To be an empty, earthen cruse
When you tried so hard
To fill me up with every liquid that I like,
And when you want to be a wave
Coming up from the bed all crest and plumage
I've got to do my best
To tip my weight - beaches burst a seam
When you froth shorewards
And is it for fun you tilt beneath me?
On September mornings there is usually
A slight ice to be broken between us
And in the face of all this
I must request
That you do not walk out in front of my bike.

WISH

I came to you a dangerous red
It was a colourful scene
I as Diana, temptress,
You with that dull-edged pain
And then the slow perfume of your arrival
And fondling of my name, loving it,
Made life scroll out till all the wars were
Just small things down there —
Though I fought too,
Needing you on all occasions,
Midnight, evening, unflinching day,
The need maturing in my hothouse brain,
Sparked up mightly to hear you say
I was a piece with many voices,
Stepping out of my disco-dance,
Tuning out of my discordance,
Tuning slack to fit your scale,
Edging over from a tangled harmony
To feel you braid affection with my hair,
Loosening and pulling tight the thews of hair.

I would have liked
To have shed that dangerous colour
To have come to you simply.

JUNE

I lie in my own laughter under trees,
The lily flexes in the shade,
Bluebells show me
How to be delicate.
It is this simplicity
That drops into my uncoloured soul
And brings the troubled whispers
Swirling to my head.
When the sands shift
I know
That this is where I have built my home.

Water is an ancient, lovely sound
I hold in my ears
Making river beds of my hands and arms
Till the sun draws it, and I find
It is only hours to June,
While in the back of my mind
December still plays
Her inky icicle-tune.

CHIMAERA

The first excitement is loosed and roams aimlessly
The skin of it wrinkling, as in a slight breeze,
It comes to them suddenly
How there is this great divide
And staring into it
They see reflections of the day they met
She was loosely bound, she was silver-skinned
And when the water turned
She was the slightest streak of rapture with the tide.
He was older, stood aside
And in the moment she was still
His glance settled in the crook of her arm,
A question darkly circling her wrist,
Each of his thoughts so clear it hung
Droplet-like.

How lightly clothed such passions go —
She flamed
He was the smouldering core
She felt his eyes on her
It gave her grace
It cleared the air
There were no barriers any more.

Now there is this great divide
All the shared things sit ill
And it comes to them, blunt as a muffled bell
How the first excitement, held against the light
'Shreds into the slightest passion of them all.

A DAY IN A SMALL TOWN

The path down a secret gets familiar, worn,
When I turn, it is there,
Nestling;
And I can exult in coming close to him
Then drawing back; to keep the secret fine
I must be able to walk easily away.
I shall loose it, like freeing a handsome bird
Into the burnt, leaf-choked air of a small town
Where we once spent a sun-tossed day,
Drawing our song with a stick down a wooden fence,
Making a song I could never forget,
Sun coming right into the car
Fusing the two of us. I would not
Pull the visor down
Though the small-town sun was blinding us
And it's a marble calm
That tombs the secret love;
My wings give a soft beat or two
Waiting to free it,
Like loosing a handsome bird.

LAUNDRETTE

The harbour town is washed with dirty greens
I hum an old lullaby until it hurts
And the dim lines of poplar trees
Breathe in time to the breaking
And the healing of the sea.
I find the slatted comfort of the wooden seats,
Sit facing the machines
Watching them digest their wet, cotton meals
And through the tumbling heat
His shirts grasp feebly at the glass door,
Dancing for me, pleading with me,
So I concentrate
Until the helpless linen tells how heavily his life lies,
How he wakes late to feel the dark come down,
Obliterate the comfort of old things, childhood things,
Long put away, dust-mantled;
And I try to fold something more
Into the warm damp of clean clothes —
Something he will come upon,
Intent in that unguarded moment
Leaning back to catch the second sleeve,
Something blue-green,
Or all the colours of a child's wish.

MOTHER

There's a downpour in the village,
Mud like porridge,
We shelter;
Outside the windows, all that winter
Hangs there, owl-like,
And our differences lift, like fog lifting
And our hearts turn, golden for a moment,
This is the house where she mothers —
No-one else casts this comfort.

She mothers the whole village,
She makes you think
Of a duck-mother, with her webbed concern,
Spreading matter-of-fact, lifebled,
Hurting love.

A consolation of children
Clutters her mealtime, paces her world
There can be no untruth for them, no pretence,
On Sundays she decks them in mother-of-pearl
She holds them when they fall
From the apple trees, from grace,
She dims the shock of skinned knees.

The rain is over.
Under the paling fence
Time huddles, waiting, as we say goodbye.

THE SWING

The afternoon's awry, it slivers off in curves
My dress makes a crimson pendant
At the garden's throat; I swing
Causing a frivolous shiver of green
Across the lawn; I am cradled there
Printing this crescent I wear
Across the brilliant, livid-sided air.
All this swinging stirs the blood,
Makes whole the filled-up heart,
Until the garden, stiff in its joints,
Begins to make fluid the swing to good
And the return to wrong
And when I fall, just let me lie
For the more I try to be featherlight
The heavier I become
And the more I try to be winged and sleepless
The heavier grow my eyes; my senses list
To the warp of the earth
Whose voice is this
Singing the swing to rest,
Shrouding it in loveliness?

II

HOME-MOVIE NIGHTS

Ratcheted, in stills,
How thin and brown the smooth-limbed
Brothers, throwing off their casts of sand
(Bury me! I am a dead man!)
Framed In loose rolls of celluloid
And I, smaller even than the buried ones
Up there on our sitting-room wall.
I was once caught under a giant wave
They brought me out alive
(They did not save my life
For I was saved on celluloid)
But through the wave I saw them dive for me
All my life they brought me, pearl-like, from the waves
And now, well used to handling the names
Of men long gone from me and unfamiliar grown
And opening the letters home
I do most of my
Wringing of hands
Alone.

LOVE OF THE DOG

I get bored with the afternoon,
It is empty of love.

"Let them do it. Let them bury the dog;"
My brothers dug
Down till the earth clung to the earth.
My father ordered the scattered death.

I visit the evening
There is no love there; in the sitting-room
Saint-Saëns mocks the human voice
With his oboe-ache
There's a light violin tread on the stairs
Organ groans drown the cellar
The whole house shelters the symphony
Flutes roost in the eaves
But all Saint-Saëns cannot dull
The dog's dying screams
Pulling strings, jarring the veins —
My brothers dug
Till earth clung whimpering to the earth
We could see very clearly all around
The furious blind-spot of the dog's death
We dug quite lucidly,
Spade-edges hovering
Dangerously close to the roots
That, touched, would have sprung us,
Strangled us.

THREE BOYS WITH FIRE

This is the old water tower
Lowering out of a gaunt dark, a dull giant
Leering dully at the stars
And here are three boys with fire;
They have kept the sounds of the day
Tangled in their pockets
Among the fishing hooks and catapult stones
And have stolen into this late hour
Spooling their shadows from a wrapping of fire.

Too much love strangles the simple vision
And if I am to be hurt
      somewhere in the middle distance
I have no apprehension.
Where fire is tapering into the dark
Trees find startling relief
And things are clearer in the light
Of three boys balancing fire with night.

EMILY DICKINSON

From anything that touches her she may recoil
Go no further
But retreat upon it all and reap
Words that are born and unfurl under careful hands
Words that come from her trance
In a silent monotone.

Then the Alice-like fall
Swings from dull thud to thud of her hitting earth.
In her long descent did she howl?
I worry about that sound
And watch how her own nouns
        jostle her now she is down,
Her thoughts are an empty train, doors open,
And no-one getting in.

At times she has nodded drily at the abyss
It is not sunny at this time so there are no shadows
But maybe down there genius lightly spirals,
Words landing squarely, perfect fits;
I edge warily, all blows glancing,
Until my mind connects with a bright shock.
Somewhere, a train pulls off.

DUCHESS

"Cover her face:mine eyes dazzle: she died young"
The Duchess of Malfi

It is your gift, and you are
Wound with it, duchess,
More white than colour can express,
Arced with it
You cast a thin wake
Widening to your own face,
Blanched, miracle of the hue
Gentles you, white and thinking
Things that were thought since time woke.
You are bound in white, rotate,
Thinning into silhouette,
The shrill pirouette scares music
Up into a hurried blur
And starts a flock
To the shivering beat of wings
That gathers to the settling of a tree
Drawing on a cloak of birds
With their brief stillness for its weave.
Wrought with it, duchess,
You put the colour in white things
And earth back on its steady keel
No crowd of shades to rush the hour
Or jog the pale meniscus in the vein.
Just white washing slightly against grey.

I DON'T WANT HIS NAME IN HERE

At his death they cried that way,
The sun howled, rain came,
I loved the grief, it had so many parts,
I hugged it to me on cold days
When the air was full
And love took longer
To recall.
His image is burned on my retina
I get dry-throated whenever I look,
I whistle in the dark,
I haven't a hope.
But light flocks, circling, and dawn
Brings soft shapes pacing in an upper room,
Maybe it will snow
Big, forgetful flakes blunting the grass
And the edge of hurt;
I don't want his name in here
But I don't regret,
I turn the death over on my palm
It is a small, soulful thing,
It could blow away.

THE KILL

Everything gets trampled on and crushed
The great wild animal in the shrieking undergrowth
Breaks his own spirit as he goes.

A man in white trousers and a polo shirt
Scuffs up little thrills of dirt,
In his hand the gun
Salivates oil,
Gorged with bullets, jawing them, ready to spit,
And down the sights of it the wild one
Circles hugely,
Measuring the iris of the hunter's eye
Nuzzling bluntly the blind instinct to survive.

Bring on the fleet, metal death,
Bring it to the heart - accurate,
Let the hooves kick in simple, clean defeat,
And the gun rest, satiate.

IN ONE BLOW

A grain of sand
Lodged between brain and skull
I couldn't think without it pearling,
Microscopic, multiplying,
It rubbed raw against the memory
Of those dunes throwing scarves into the wind,
The lit sand billowing like a yellow mist
Blurred with the promise of rain.
I was on the edge of the earth
Now and again
A tree showed skeletal in the void
Dried out by despair,
There was nothing out there, and in one blow
I could have lost all that held my happiness down,
Pinned to the ground, flapping
In the sand-stricken wind.

I felt grains gather at the artery walls,
Huddled against the flow, the swell,
Fat cells squeezed through the hourglass valves,
The shifting sand
Was time measured, flowing and dammed,
And in the desert heat the blood flowered,
The stamens powdered with sand.
I felt grains shadow my lashes —
I shook them out with the promise of tears.

THE MASS IS OVER

The mass is over, they have gone in peace
but wind flays the church's sides
I fear my frail cover will be blown
Despite the sunlight on confessional doors,
Desultory coins,
The urgent reaching of the women's prayers.

I have taken refuge from a bitter shower
And find myself at Christ's fire
Yearning for things I've had
And won't have again
Because I have done wrong.
He passes - and a shudder of sparks
Ignites the recognition,
A dark object in a field of light
Where I have come for shelter
In the warm eye of the wind.

III

A TIME OF DROUGHT

I am with you on the long road
I keep time
With your pale and winded giving in,
I don't let go.
Today I shared a day long lifting of the weight
We water-skiied at a warm place
We pitched in
Learning the feel,
I saw your shoulders straighten
      with the load removed,
You held tight to your nerve,
Riding the surf,
Laughing your ropeworn laugh —
I thought you'd rise above the mounting dread,
Your child's shrinking from the end of things,
But you were sinking, anchored at the wrists,
Head bent to those depths
Plumbed from an early age.
I watched the water rise against your dry sides,
I saw it suited you to drown,
My heart kicked up enough sand to hide itself
And lie back still, for you scorn places
Where the rock-falls make a shallow pool;
You held tight to your fraying nerve,
You took hold of my words,
They came by the roots
As in a time of drought.

CLOSED OUT

I saw you close me out with that one look
The flick of a smile-edge emptied ash
In a sad flutter
Down
And I am only some dull creature
       thudding softly round
Not pretty, though gentle and so
Unwitting, treading white snow brown,
Bewildered by you
Burning through the trees like a whipping wind
Silver-witted
While I am slow iron
And when you opened my hand
And found the first bloom
Wincing from a late frost, on the palm,
Winter fled through the air in a fine dust
Making me feel I end soon too
Now you have closed me out with no word.

THE GIRL WHO WENT TO LIVE ON A WALL

I am sorry you went,
Hands spread wide, fingers delicate,
To live on your wall; hopeless before all
Advice; needing no consent.
You could fall
And nothing would break.

See how the stones lie quietly together.
In the morning, out of a purple-bruise sky
Lemon sun Lemons each one;
        stones turning to each other
Humbled by their lying together.

Today is the first day you have not seen
The sun rise; I need only your eyes
To see to the writing of these difficult words
Feelings trapped between the
Lines, speared on the i's and fluttering.

I only held you for that brief moment
As you pecked the grain of truth
And flew.

MAKER OF RAIN

I hear the muffled voice of my heart
The fretted moan,
When the day sinks to its knees
All full of cries and heavy skied
And I know
You still have the power you had
When we slept in the dim room.

When we came in late
Full of the labour of sun-down
And dropping dark,
Drawn close by the doors creaking under our skin
And the cats brushing, saucer-eyed, against the dark,
How you wove the threads of me
Into slumbering cloth.

I answer the voice of coming rain
With words of the sunlogged room
Where we lay until late in the afternoon
You still have that steady hand —
Opening my sorrow
Wide as it will go,
Maker of rain
I ghost the intimate room
Where you wove the sheen of my most precious moods
And I know
You still have the power you had
When we slept in that dim room.

INTO THIS GENTLENESS

Coming from your severity
Into this gentleness
You run your voice along our slender bond
Touching on movements of our animal son
And his instinct - knowing of winter.

I am bullied by the sudden thought
That nothing has been learned.
Frightened, over the child's head,
I see you in light thrown
By this father-boy comparison,
And in the careless shrug is offered
Yolk of the man
Offered to me in the sideways glance
And in the phrase you cannot end.

The Liffey runs full-bellied
Under the sighs of many arches
The motor idles
And, seeing me unhappy without grace,
Without veiled sorrow,
Your fingers touch my nape
You rest one word in my ear's hollow
And that's enough.

THE FIGURES IN THE RAIN

Over all the flowers I hold
You have sometime bent your head, inhaled
My peony's bluff soul
My violent rose.
And every time your train goes
My life lies fallow about the tracks
Like bramble whips
The small blind winds blow dark without you
I try opening colours to wander through
But you so briefly visit everything I own,
Sing to me of the meek figures in the rain,
Then leave with the scent of my scarlet blooms
Still colouring you. Sing me the song again
Of the meek figures
For there is often rain,
Tell me the story of the figures of doubt
Then bend your head and depart,
Leaving me to wring from my heart how
If I had come from the dark,
If I had only looked up
From the dark crook of my arm
Life could have been so warm
And I could have seen so much.

THE DROWNING ELEMENT

He leans to her with his red liar's hand
Under the swelling cotton she carries the second child
No longer trusting him —
The small head movements as she sews
Mute assurance that the child grows —
Smiling, and not trusting him at all.

So little beauty to it now,
He treads the eggshell joy
And when it is time for the right word
And he misunderstands, as she had known he would,
She smiles, and lays one hand flat
Over the bruise
Watching it spread like a stain
At the hottest part of the day;
Coming up for air
To a place where there is always water,
Surfacing to a black place,
That colour flocking to her hair,
Her eyes, the clothes she wears.

Returning late, he pours the dregs of his day
Into her lap
Until he has spilled out every drop,
She shakes it out into the dying fire
And meets the dark of the bedroom with her own dark
Aware he is blind to the drowning element in things,
Minnowing down through a pool of sleep
To a deep rest on the rock bed.

DEATH OF A RED FLOWER

I am not clear today, there's a bloom on me,
You've got gentle hands and I may cry again
For you replenished that unhappy reservoir,
That lake we found, hugging in on itself.
Even our silent awe sent ripples
To the other shore.

You discard things as you understand them.
After ten years you know well
How a whole parcel of your life
May be bound tight and put up on a shelf.
Memory is a red flower,
The best bloom,
Chosen by you from a drenching of colour
On a March street-corner.
Today I put it in dying water
It has lasted these ten years,
Only now is it bruising.

DO YOU?

You came for Sunday afternoon,
You stayed for tea
And look what you left behind —
Every memory, sheafed carelessly on my window seat,
Of you and someone who looks sadly,
Sadly, sadly like me.
I sometimes think I see you
Loitering in the shrubbery
Without intent, idling nonchalantly
Under the weeping beech; I sent
Those memories, lovingly enveloped, to that
Memorable attic flat,
Someday I may even
Stand at your door,
Hopeful and
Completely uncalled for;
But distance is proving such a very thick wall
I can hardly hear you any more.
Do you feel this at all? Do you?

FIVE CATS

I did not leave you.
I left your cats —
Walter, Salome, Aaron, Muriel, Z.

While I stood at the bedroom door,
Unmade,
Wondering had I faith
Enough to lose, and to lose,
They bulked out the narrow grief,
Furred it,
Silkily, I felt it against my cheek.

You left me further every ebb,
Husked, standing straight in the wind,
I would not bend
Except to send an arrow straying
From the quiver of my back
Or to bury my head
In the rarefied air
Of your not being there.

You did not leave me.
Your cats left me —
Walter, Salome, Aaron, Muriel, Z.

LOOK BACK

Feels ice-white when I wake
Sleep is blanketing the earth
And such a sky, coming in one leaden breath
Over the West —
The mist, the bracken and a bitter cleanliness —
There's a pall of November.
Won't be long before we climb
The brightly hung, needle strewn
December slopes
Into a roselit, firecoloured time.
But I'm in no mood for substitutes,
I see myself jumped to the earth,
All the common joy wrung out of me
The wintry seams of me
Unpicked with needletips.
The land is groaning under the ice
The drawn and quartered earth
Is skeleton-taut.
I will look back once, but not in sorrow,
Not in remorse, not in any of these things
But because I was one
Who always waved at trains,
At distant figures boarding planes
At anyone who might look back.

WINTERING

Of course I feel you gathering up to leave.
In our tightest, briefest arguments
I crush nettles with my blind left hand,
The child in me peers through a grid of fingers,
My eyes are an open wound.

Your lies have piranha teeth
Freshwater white,
The stones of the river grieve
Until they are worn smooth,
And pain has its way with me —
A great fish, nosing at my spine.

Because I will not try to blunt
This helpless, piercing sight
You push me to one side,
The cold air salts my face,
Perhaps this, too, is a cure,
For you are slight
And leave no trace.
My hand digests the slowest nettle juice,
I have no scars to show
But I have heard
The muttered refrain of wintering
Tremble up from a flurry of dried leaves
At your heel; it goes —
Bury me, I shall grow in Spring.

DECEMBER 1st
(For Barry)

The river was dark with Ormond Quay
And bright with the bridge,
The tenements fully drawn;
No-one stays up that late,
We were the only ones, we walked
With snow on our shoes as the month changed,
The crushed fish ice on the quays as December came,
The last change of a year growing old
With and without particular grace;
The streets tailed off to a light sleep,
Woke in the middle of our walk
To some sound; we sang,
The river trembled, it wore
Its heart so close to the air,
Heart that tasted dry and drew a tide with it,
All holidays began with it
And we weren't going home. It wasn't time

No common language but in sight —
The moon as the only thing
We both saw for sure, and it was
Neither greater nor slighter,
It's roundness spoken with a common word;
By Ringsend Docks a trench was dug
The spare earth under the tint of ink
May have been
Wet and gold, sure of growth
And of the emptiness of stone;
For half our lives there is no
Green or half-green or gold
To give the words a body and a soul.
We chose the searchlit quays
In search of an end,
Of the right home, or of a way
To keep us walking on that riverbank
Until our boat went down.

COMING TO SHORE

Having come to shore
Spring is down where the first wave is
Always breaking,
Hems a little damp;
Beyond the sand
It shrugs off a winter coat
From those buttonholes sprout
New grasses,
Crocuses.
Further in,
Leaves are details on a creamy shirt.
A garment next to the skin,
Each thread a flowerhead,
Bluish tips,
Throbbing stalks,
A dream of Spring was carrier of their seed;
It's time to count on frost,
Expect it
Timed and ticking in a whorled shell,
Thrown on the shore,
Dragged there without reason
To bruise this season at the roots.

CONVALESCENT

There's smoke in the air although it's Spring,
People are shedding muddy boots and things,
Slamming their private doors
On rooms with sofas and TVs,
I fall into the wind
It rights me, mildly,
And I walk like a convalescent
Down a tree-lined path,
Wood-soothed, thinking of bough
And bark and all that will come
Of the nutshell,
The circles in the circles
That the lathe handles lovingly
With its gaze,
The hacked limb a lumberman heals
With his dab of bright paint.
Somewhere friends are waiting,
Lies in their hands,
Hands by their sides.

THE HUNG MAN

I have hung, spider-kicking
Between laughter and fine sorrow
When this happens I drink coffee and I
Don't know what to do.

From the top of the world
Every slope runs down.
I'd hate to die right now —
I have this scent between skin and bone,
It smells of a nightmare town
That knows no primary colour.

You have no idea what it's like
To hang with hope and a fear of falling,
It is strange and strong
How the thoughts run
Where limbs won't go;
I am taking the winter sun
On the backs of my hands,
Pleased I am not of the dead ones,
I am safer now than I have ever been
But sometimes you just feel
Unclean.

SINGLE VISION
(For Liam)

I close one eye, I cannot allow
Two perspectives on this man
Not even two. Across the room
He looks at me, full-eyed,
My other lovers cloud across my brain
Memory lies when there are no faces here
This knowledge sends tight hands to play
      a minor strain
In an orchestra of nerves, up and down
Up and down my fretted spine.
It plays a painted post on a black mountain road
It plays a broken arrow by a walled lake,
      Battle Creek,
That shows a landscape fiddled to the bone
All the slow juice of orchards
Rivuleting down stone of Cherry Hill
And watering the jowls
Of Half Moon Bay. These are the names
I met him by, his name has an L,
I am moulded by that letter, it spells lover,
Life-giver.

THE COURAGE GATHERER

With the sun too close
A loose wind catches me off guard,
Dreams flock to my skirts
And cling there like a litter
I'd steal sleep to feed.
Asked exactly how I feel
I answer from the fields and summer lanes
Where I have come
Gathering courage.
A wing shadow strobes the lane
From time to time the future sinks
With the black doubt of people leaving me —
But hope comes out in her lovely shimmer,
Her hair behind, untied,
Fresh on the morning, never fully woken,
Never still.
I follow with my arms full
Of the songs she leaves,
All of the same brave tune.